THE GAP IN THE PERCEPTION OF THE BUSINESS VALUE OF DESIGN

THE GAP IN THE PERCEPTION OF THE BUSINESS VALUE OF DESIGN

Jasmin Roth

GALDA VERLAG 2024

Bibliografische Information der Deutschen Nationalbibliothek
Die Deutsche Nationalbibliothek verzeichnet diese Publikation in der Deutschen Nationalbibliografie; detaillierte bibliografische Daten sind im Internet über https://dnb.de abrufbar.

© 2024 Galda Verlag, Glienicke
Neither this book nor any part may be reproduced or transmitted in any form or by any means electronic or mechanical, including photocopying, micro-filming, and recording, or by any information storage or retrieval system, without prior permission in writing from the publisher. Direct all inquiries to:
Galda Verlag, Franz-Schubert-Str. 61, 16548 Glienicke, Germany

Originally presented as the author's thesis (masteral):
Vienna University of Economics and Business, 2023

ISBN 978-3-96203-372-9 (Print)
ISBN 978-3-96203-373-6 (E-Book)

ABBREVIATIONS

List of abbreviations

CDO	Chief Design Officer
DMI	Design Management Institute
DVI	Design Value Index
EVA	Economic Value Added
IP	Intellectual Property
IP 1–8	Interview Partner 1–8
KPI	Key Performance Indicator
MBA	Master of Business Administration
MS	Microsoft
R&D	Research & Development
ROI	Return on Investment
SMEs	Small and medium-sized enterprises
S&P 500	Standard & Poor's 500
TQM	Total Quality Management
TV	Television
UI	User Interface
UX	User Experience

LIST OF FIGURES AND TABLES

Figures

Fig. 1. Visualization of the "perception gap" between designers and non-designers

Fig. 2. Visualization of the four stakeholders who have an impact on the "perception gap"

Fig. 3. Findings of the results added to the visualization of the four stakeholders who have an impact on the "perception gap"

Tables

Tab. 1. Design management is defined by what you think of design (vertical axis: the "learning ladder" of design), and by what you think of management (horizontal axis). Table after Borja de Mozota (2006).

Tab. 2. Overview of interview partners (IP 1–8)

TABLE OF CONTENTS

CHAPTER ONE: INTRODUCTION

A. Problem formulation 13
B. Terminology 13
C. Objectives and research questions 14
D. Course of investigation 14
E. Contribution of this research 16

CHAPTER TWO: LITERATURE PART

A. Design within the design realm 17
    I. The challenge of framing design 17
    II. Non-designers perceive design differently than designers do 18
    III. The importance of design is on the rise 19
B. Design within the management realm 20
    I. Strategic relevance of design 20
    II. Design in established strategy frameworks 21
C. The "perception gap" 24
    I. Origins of and reasons for the "perception gap" 24
    II. Four stakeholders and their impact on the "perception gap" 29

CHAPTER THREE:
EMPIRICAL PART

A. Methodology 33
B. Research Design 33
    I. Survey period 33
    II. Survey approach 35
    III. Selection criteria for the interview partners 35
    IV. Guiding interview questions 35

CHAPTER FOUR:
RESULTS AS AGGREGATED FEEDBACK

A. Perspectives on the relationship between designer and manager (non-designer) 37
B. Perspectives on the ability of design to contribute value to a business 39
C. Perspectives on the pain points in the cooperation between designer and manager (non-designer) 41
D. Perspectives on how an ideal designer-manager-relationship could look like 45
E. Perspectives on ways to overcome the "perception gap" 45
F. Expectations of designers and managers (non-designer) towards representatives 48
G. Expectations of representatives towards each other or a third-party 50

CHAPTER FIVE:
DISCUSSION AND INTERPRETATION

A. The mutual perception of designers and managers (non-designers) 53

    I. The designer-manager-relationship 53

    II. The power of design 54

B. The key pain points that contribute to the misunderstanding in communication between designers and managers (non-designers) 56

    I. Briefing for and scope of the design process 57

    II. Costs and budgets 58

    III. Trust and fear in decision-making 59

C. Overcoming the "perception gap" 61

    I. Common language and values 61

    II. Getting expectations right 62

    III. Education on both sides 62

D. The mutual expectations of designers, managers (nondesigners) and representatives 63

    I. Designers demand true representation and a re-definition of the design profession 63

    II. Managers demand access to design for SMEs and an integration of design into business education and vice versa 64

    III. Design representatives demand longer business cycles, and the support of policymakers to completely rethink school from the ground up 65

    IV. Business representatives demand more pressure to raise design awareness and hold design representatives accountable for doing the same 66

CHAPTER SIX:
CONCLUSION & FUTURE MANAGERIAL IMPLICATIONS

Conclusion & Future Managerial Implications 67

LIMITATIONS 71
REFERENCES... 73
APPENDIX 77
   A. Guiding interview questions for designers and managers (non-designers) 77
   B. Guiding interview questions for design and business representatives.. 79

CHAPTER ONE

INTRODUCTION

A. Problem formulation

This master's thesis is situated at the intersection of the design realm and the management realm. Design matters, whether a company focuses on manufacturing physical goods, digital products, services, or some combination of these (Sheppard et al., 2018). However, the business value of design is often perceived differently by designer and manager (non-designer), leading to a significant gap in understanding and appreciation (Chiang et al., 2019). It is this misperception that prevents design from developing and delivering its full potential. This master's thesis aims to address this gap in perception and builds upon the author's observation and experience as a designer in the creative industries over a span of more than fifteen years.

As there is hardly any literature on the perception of the business value of design available (Landoni et al., 2016, Howden and Pressey, 2008), this research aims to analyze the status quo, to name and identify underlying drivers and lay a foundation for future research. Through a comprehensive review of existing literature and insightful interviews with experts, the complex relationship between designer and manager (non-designer) will be explored and possible ways to enhance mutual understanding and build common ground identified.

B. Terminology

A designer is defined as a highly skilled individual who operates within the creative industries. They are professionals who bring their creative expertise and specialized knowledge to solve problems strategically, create visually appealing and functional solutions, and communicate ideas effectively through various media.

In the context of this thesis, a manager is defined as an individual who does not possess a formal design background (non-designer) but is actively involved in making decisions related to design aspects. They may hold positions such as entrepreneurs running their own business, marketing managers, or other similar roles where they collaborate with designers to shape design elements such as branding, positioning, website development, and more.

C. Objectives and research questions

This thesis aims to investigate the gap in the perception of the business value of design between designer and manager (non-designer) by answering the following research questions:

> Q1: *How do designer and manager (non-designer) perceive each other?*
> Q2: *What are the key pain points that contribute to the misunderstanding in communication between designer and manager (non-designer)?*
> Q3: *How can the "perception gap" be overcome?*
> Q4: *What is expected from representatives?*

The goal of this thesis is to present a comprehensive and nuanced picture of the current state of the designer-manager-relationship. By identifying pain points and exploring the layers of the perception gap it aims to lay the groundwork for future research and initiatives or improve ongoing efforts that can contribute to bridging the gap and fostering a more effective and harmonious relationship between designer and manager (non-designer). A better mutual understanding would bring benefits to both sides. The designer would feel better understood, and the managers could fully harness the potential of design for their purposes.

D. Course of investigation

To answer the research questions, this thesis consists of a literature part and an empirical part. The literature part recognizes the limited existing literature and undertakes a comprehensive analysis. In a first step it is explored how design is perceived within the design realm versus the management realm. In a second step the differences in perception, underlying reasons for that and affected stakeholder groups are investigated.

Following a Grounded Theory approach (Strauss and Corbin, 1997), the empirical part will consist of eight qualitative, semi-structured expert interviews. Guiding interview questions (Appendix A, B) will establish a thread throughout the conversations. Spontaneous follow up questions are aiming for valuable insights to get the fullest possible picture of the current situation. In order to gain a comprehensive understanding of the broader implications and challenges surrounding the perception gap between designer and manager (non-designer), it is important to engage not only with designers and managers (non-designers) but also with industry and education representatives. Restricting the dialogue solely to designer and manager would be short-sighted and limit the potential for a holistic perspective on the matter.

Designer and manager bring unique expertise and firsthand experiences that are very relevant in understanding the nuances and dynamics of the designer-manager-relationship. Designers possess deep knowledge and expertise in their craft, enabling them to provide valuable insights into the creative process, day-to-day realities from success to frustration, design thinking, and the impact of design on user experience. Their perspective helps to uncover the hurdles of design implementation, the challenges they face in conveying the value of design to managers, and their aspirations for the future of the design profession. On the other hand, managers offer a distinct viewpoint rooted in their experience of leading and overseeing business operations. Their understanding of organizational dynamics and strategic decision-making can provide insights into the challenges they face in integrating design into business strategies, articulating the value of design to stakeholders, and aligning design objectives with broader business goals.

Industry representatives, such as professional associations, industry organizations, and chambers of commerce, also play a significant role in shaping the designer-manager relationship. These groups represent the collective interests of businesses and can provide a platform for dialogue, collaboration, and advocacy.

Similarly, education representatives contribute crucial insights into the training and development of the future designer and manager and shed light on opportunities to enhance design and business education in order to bridge the perception gap.

This multi-stakeholder approach ensures that the research findings and recommendations consider the viewpoints and experiences of key actors involved in the design and business ecosystem, fostering a more holistic understanding of the bigger picture at hand.

E. Contribution of this research

This master's thesis contributes to the existing literature by filling a gap in the understanding of the business value of design and the relationship between designers and managers. It lays a foundation for future research by analyzing the current status quo, identifying underlying drivers, and highlighting areas for improvement. The author's professional background adds a unique dimension to the research, offering valuable insights into the daily challenges faced by designers, unnoticed potentials of value creation through design, and consequently, avenues for future exploration.

This research expands the discussion on the value of design beyond the traditional focus on designers and managers to include designers, managers, and their representatives. The author advocates for adopting a four-forces perspective to collaborate effectively, elevate the profession of designers, and enhance overall design awareness.

CHAPTER TWO

LITERATURE PART

This literature review is situated on the intersection of the design realm and the management realm and focuses on how the business value of design is perceived. It looks at the understanding of the design profession in general and explores reasons for the discrepancies in the perception of the business value of design.

A. Design within the design realm

I. The challenge of framing design

There are several challenges in understanding design, including its multidisciplinary nature, the subjectivity of design evaluations, and the difficulty in measuring its impact. First, design is a multidisciplinary field, drawing on psychology, engineering, and aesthetics among others. This can make it difficult to fully understand the various factors that contribute to design and how they interact (Cross, 2023).

Victor Papanek, author of *Design for the Real World* describes the multifaceted character of design as *"All that we do, almost all the time, is design, for design is basic to all human activity. The planning and patterning of any act towards a desired, foreseeable end constitutes the design process. Any attempt to separate design, to make it a thing-by-itself, works counter to the fact that design is the primary underlying matrix of life. Design is composing an epic poem, executing a mural, painting a masterpiece, writing a concerto. But design is also cleaning and reorganizing a desk drawer, pulling an impacted tooth, baking an apple, choosing sides for a backlot baseball game, and educating a child"* (Papanek and Lazarus, 2020: 3).

Second, the evaluation of the quality of design is often subjective, as it often comes with personal preferences and is often judged by non-designers. This makes it challenging to develop objective criteria for evaluating design and leads to disagreements about the quality of a design solution (Cross, 2023). While designers have a tendency to argue in terms of the impact of the design process or value contribution to culture, non-designers often talk in the categories of personal taste and numbers.

Third, it is difficult to measure the impact of design on business outcomes. While there is evidence that design can drive innovation and increase customer satisfaction, it can be challenging to quantify the specific impact that design has on a business's bottom line (Stevens et al., 2008).

One could ask in general what is meant when the term "design" is used in a conversation? When people talk about the design of the iPhone, the design of a company's logo or design thinking the context and meaning of the term "design" varies a lot.

"The word 'design' means different things to different people. Depending on their point of view [...]" (Lorenz, 1994: 73). Besides having different meanings in different types of contexts, design is also perceived differently by designers and non-designers. Especially regarding the understanding of the design profession and the value or impact it can provide.

Simon London, host of "The McKinsey Podcast", even calls design the fuzziest word in the business dictionary (Sheppard et al., 2018). In conversation with the McKinsey partners Ben Sheppard and Hyo Yeon design is defined with regard to three aspects:

1. Design as a craft
2. Design as a process
3. Design as an end-product or service

II. Non-designers perceive design differently than designers do

In the general public, design is often misunderstood, since designers are widely perceived as 'stylists', 'decorators', 'craftsmen', or 'artisans', who primarily work towards the goal of making things look beautiful (Muratovski, 2010). As noted by Short (2011), such generalized perceptions limit the progress of acceptance of e.g. graphic design as a true profession, as it is assumed that graphic designers have lighter responsibilities (Cheung, 2012) – On the contrary, graphic design offers a wide field of action in various scales and responsibilities as Chiang et al. describe: *"From the design of a single business card to a whole series of brand identity system, or from a company's website to the print and digital advertisements of an integrated advertising campaign, graphic design can take place at any scale and any time"* (Chiang et al., 2019: 1).

In contrast to the public in general, designers, design scholars, and international design associations view design as a strategic tool that can bring enormous values towards businesses, markets, societies, and economies around the world. Design can be used meaningfully to produce various forms of effective solutions for products, and services, but also intangibles such as strategy and experiences. (Muratovski, 2021, Bennett, 2011)

III. The importance of design is on the rise

Regarding the design profession, there are three important trends of recent decades to note. First, Nussbaum highlights the importance of design's ability to differentiate products and services in a global market. He argues that good design is the last remaining competitive differentiator, when high quality is becoming a standard and affordable, even commoditized (Nussbaum, 2004), design can make the experience feel very different.

Second, the recognition of design's importance has been more and more widely acknowledged. It started with Kotler and Rath in 1984, as they urged business leaders to view design in a broader sense instead of limiting it to a decorative add-on that is applied in a late stage of development (Stevens et al., 2008, Kotler and Alexander Rath, 1984). Four realms of design's contribution – value, image, process, and production – were identified by Trueman and Jobbler. This underlined that if managers only recognize design in the area to improve a company's visual image, they will miss out on the advantages of the other three (Trueman and Jobber, 1998). Seidel (2000) introduces four strategic areas of contribution that are positively affected by working with a design consultant (visualizing and communicating strategy, recognizing unseen market opportunities, matching competencies dispersed through the organization, providing design process guidance). This trend can also be observed in a shift of the designer's profession, as many design agencies enlarge their scope of work with consulting services.

Third, in academia the examination of the value of product design is a long standing one. More recent thinking focuses on design's broader contribution to operations and business success outside of manufacturing (Stevens et al., 2008).

B. Design within the management realm

In management literature, the importance of design is being increasingly recognized and many researchers support the thesis that design, and more specifically investments in design, positively influence the business results of firms (Borja de Mozota, 2006, Landoni et al., 2016, Stevens et al., 2008, Dumas and Mintzberg, 1991, Gorb and Dumas, 1987, Moultrie et al., 2006, Kotler and Alexander Rath, 1984).

The way managers perceive design depends on two things: First, to what degree they are non-designers themselves. Especially Stevens et al. (2008) consider a view based on strategy as an entrepreneur's personal vision. Second, how knowledgeable they are when it comes to management literature, where the value contribution of design is widely acknowledged (Borja de Mozota, 2006, Landoni et al., 2016, Stevens et al., 2008, Dumas and Mintzberg, 1991, Gorb and Dumas, 1987, Moultrie et al., 2006, Kotler and Alexander Rath, 1984, Kramoliš and Staňková, 2017).

I. Strategic relevance of design

Stevens et al. (2008) suggest that design's strategic relevance can be considered in three ways:

1. Competing by "high design" as a strategic position
2. Using an integrated, coherent design approach to implement strategic positioning
3. Utilization of design methods to inform strategy formulation

In their work, they looked at established strategy frameworks within the management realm from a design perspective and connected the contribution of design to Porter's Generic Strategies Framework, The Five Forces and The Value Chain.

Borja de Mozota (2006) speaks of four strategic roles of design:

1. Design as differentiator
2. Design as integrator
3. Design as transformer
4. Design as good business

Borja de Mozota (2006) connects design to Porter's frameworks as well and suggests to demonstrate the value of design by the economic-value-added (EVA) framework and to capture it with the Balanced Score Card model.

She points out that what a person thinks design is capable of doing is defined by what a person thinks of design (depending on their individual progress on the "learning ladder" of design) and by what a person thinks about management.

Management literature mentions two phenomena that are highly relevant for this thesis – *silent design* (Gorb and Dumas, 1987) and *silent design in reverse* (Stevens et al., 2008). *Silent design* covers all contributions to a design process that come from non-designers and are therefore not acknowledged as design (Gorb and Dumas, 1987). It is design or support activities by e.g. managers who are not designers and are not aware that they are participating in design activity (Dumas and Mintzberg, 1991).

In contrast to that, *silent design in reverse* refers to the invisible contribution of design professionals to business success. Enhancing performance in so called "non-design areas" is often unacknowledged. (Stevens et al., 2008)

To demonstrate the value design contributes to business performance, the Design Management Institute (DMI) developed *The Design Value Index* (DVI) (DMI, 2013). This is a widely recognized tool to measure the financial performance of companies that prioritize design. The DVI measures the stock performance of companies that are identified as design driven and compares it to the S&P 500 index over a 10-year period. Specifically, the report found that design-driven companies outperformed the S&P 500 by a factor of 2.11 between 2013 and 2019. A company is considered design-driven if they have a chief design officer (CDO) or equivalent role, or if they have design integrated throughout the organization in a systematic way.

The DVI does not provide a direct measure of the value of design but is rather a proof of concept which suggests that if companies invest in design as a strategic asset they tend to perform better financially. The DVI is therefore a tool to visualize the positive long-term effect of strategic and integrated design.

Overall, it is a big challenge to quantify the value of design. In the following, design is connected to established strategy frameworks in order to get an overview of manager's potential touchpoints with design.

II. Design in established strategy frameworks

Both Stevens et al. (2008) and Borja de Mozota (2002, 2006) refer to Porter's established strategy concepts of differentiation and positioning.

Therefore, in the following it will be reviewed how design is related to Porter's Generic Strategies Framework, The Five Forces and The Value Chain.

Porter's Generic Strategies Framework (Porter, 1996) outlines three generic types of strategy that companies can use to position themselves in the marketplace: *cost leadership, differentiation,* and *focus.*

According to Stevens et al. (2008), design plays its most obvious and visible role in *differentiation*, as protection against competitors through perceived uniqueness. For Borja de Mozota (2002) this is the main reason why companies engage external design experts in the first place. As the conception and specification of desirable products and services is in general perceived as a designer's main competence.

Regarding *cost leadership* Stevens et al. (2008) point out design's ambivalent role. Companies pursuing a cost leadership strategy aim to achieve the lowest possible cost of production in their industry. On the one hand, design can act at product level with a focus on efficiency and cost saving through process design and design for manufacture. On the other hand, it can help in communicating a cost leadership position. Here Stevens et al. (2008) refer to Moultrie et al. (2006) who found that this function of design is not always recognized, as in a company that aims for minimizing all costs, design might be seen as an unnecessary and unjustifiable expense.

Design can also be a valuable tool to sharpen the third dimension*focus.* As noted by Brown (2008), designers use their skills in empathy and understanding to identify the unique needs of a particular market segment and design products or services that meet those needs. This aspect is obviously closely related to *differentiation.*

When thinking about design's value in manipulating the forces at play outside of an organization, Porter's Five Forces must be revisited (Porter, 1985). Porter defines five competitive dynamics of an industry: the threat of new entrants, the bargaining power of suppliers, the bargaining power of buyers, the threat of substitute products or services, and the intensity of rivalry among existing competitors.

According to Stevens et al. (2008) customer loyalty is important in three out of five forces, reducing the customer's probability to switch to rivals, new entrants or substitutes. He continues that, as it is one of design's core competences to meet customer needs with appealing products and experiences reinforced with a strong image and brand identity, it has the ability to strengthen customer loyalty.

In terms of competitive price wars and profit-cutting strategies, design enables a company to rise above the competition within the market.

Besides that, design in combination with radical distinctiveness can elevate a late-comer above an established competitor. As noted by Stevens et al., design-led strategies always bear the risk of being copied if not robustly protected through IP rights.

Regarding substitution in a very competitive market, when high quality is becoming a standard and affordable, even commoditized (Nussbaum, 2004) design can make the experience feel very different.

Supplier power can be influenced by technological design choices and the degree of dependency on partners.

Steven concludes that it is an important step towards an integrated design approach if design is viewed as a tool to shape relationships and experiences in all five of Porter's realms.

In his original framework of The Value Chain Porter only recognizes design in its technological sense, namely in 'operations' and 'technology development' (Lorenz, 1994). Stevens et al. show how design can be an integrated support activity in the value chain, spanning all primary operations (inbound logistics, operations, outbound logistics, marketing and sales, and service). Therefore, design's value must be seen as a result of an integrated effort of several design specializations (graphic, interactive, industrial, etc.) across all operations.

Papers on design's place in the value chain are rare. According to Borja de Mozota (2002) it acts simultaneously at three levels as differentiator, transformer, and co-ordinator: improving primary activities by using design to raise the consumer perceived value, improving coordination among functions and the support activities by viewing design as a new function in the management process, improving the external coordination of the company by using design to generate a new vision for an industry.

Quantifying the value of design in Porter's terms is very difficult, because much of it lies within the intangible value of goods and services (Kotler and Alexander Rath, 1984). Besides that, the phenomena of *silent design* and *silent design in reverse* cause difficulties in attributing valuable contributions to either the design or management realm. Even if the designer and manager both aim for the success of the business, they might have different objectives and expectations in mind.

C. The "perception gap"

The discrepancy in the perception of design by non-designers and designers is called the "perception gap" (Chiang et al., 2019). In the context of this thesis the perception gap between designers and managers is examined (Fig. 1).

I. Origins of and reasons for the "perception gap"

Landoni et al. (2016) looked at studies that over the years have contributed to the understanding of design and identified two main barriers: the lack of a common language on design and poor analysis of the dynamics that characterize the relationship between investment in design and competitive performance. The lack of common language between design and management is a frequent issue (Gill, 1990, Micheli et al., 2012, Sebastian, 2005, Chiang et al., 2019, Gill and Graell, 2016). While both groups may strive toward a common goal, they often have different perspectives and ways of communicating.

Micheli et al. found out that organizations often face a communication gap between designer and non-designer. Designers speak in a visual language, while managers speak in a language of numbers and data. This creates a communication gap that impacts collaboration and decision-making (Micheli et al., 2012).

Sebastian agrees that a lack of common language leads to ineffective collaboration and misunderstandings. He mentions the example that designers may not fully understand the business goals and financial constraints of the organization while non-designers may not fully appreciate the value of design in achieving those goals. The design and management disciplines have different sets of skills, practices, and values. While designers focus on creativity and innovation, managers focus on strategy and financial performance. These differences can make it challenging to find common ground and achieve shared goals. (Sebastian, 2005)

The following reasons for a lack of common language between design and management have been mentioned in existing literature:

Chiang et al. mention the difference in educational and professional backgrounds. Designers may have a background in art, architecture, or engineering, while managers may have a background in business, economics, or finance. This can lead to differences in language, terminology, and ways of thinking (Chiang et al., 2019).

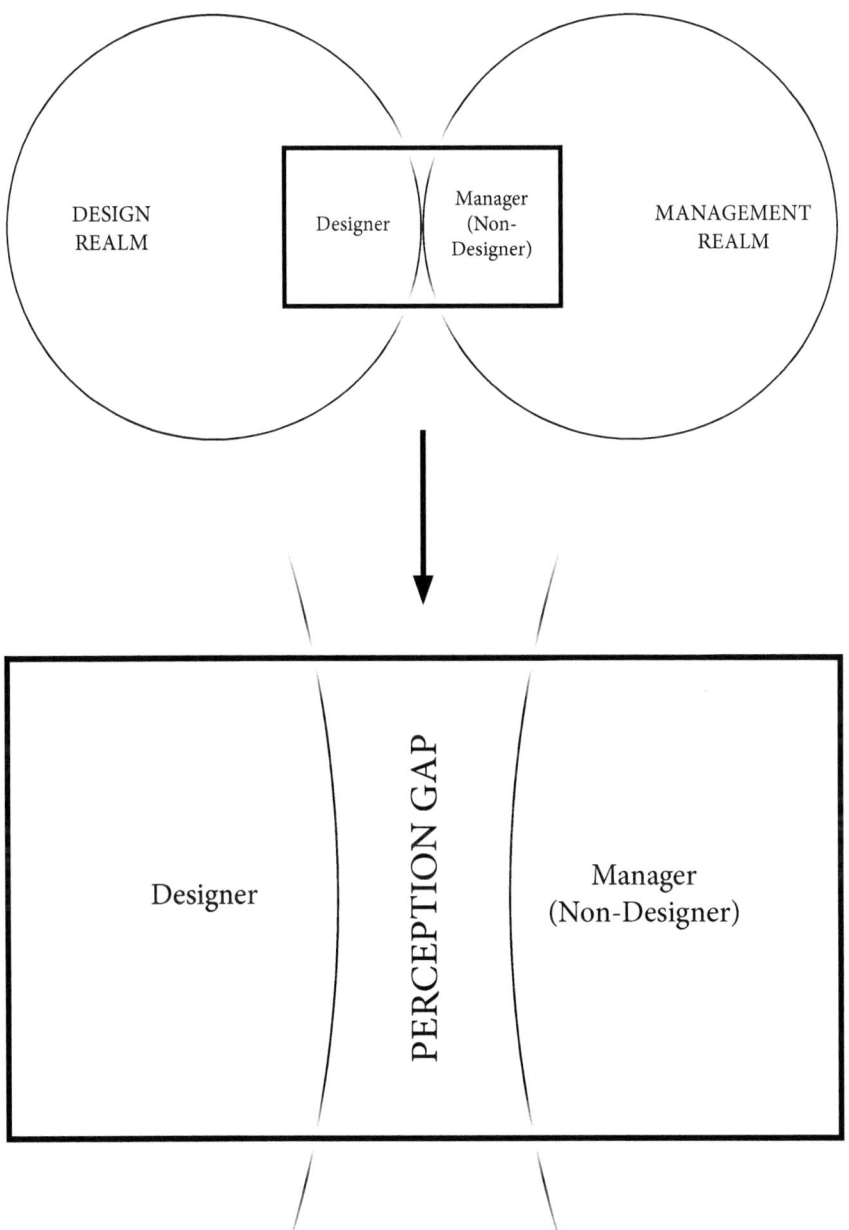

Fig. 1 Area of investigation.
Visualization of the "perception gap"
between designers and non-designers
Source: the author, 2023

Gill and Graell state that design and management are not only two different disciplines, but they are also two different cultures. Designers see things in a very different way than managers do (Gill and Graell, 2016).

Micheli et al. found that when it comes to problem-solving, designers and non-designers have different ways of approaching problems and exploring solutions. Designers rely more on intuition and creativity, while managers rely more on analysis and data. (Micheli et al., 2012).

The poor analysis of the dynamics that characterize the relationship between investment in design and competitive performance (Landoni et al., 2016) comes from the difficulty to link design investments to the bottom line.

The relationship between investment in design and competitive performance is influenced by many variables, such as the industry, the market, and the specific design activities being invested in. It can be difficult to isolate the impact of design investment from other factors that may affect competitive performance (Kramoliš and Staňková, 2017). The effects of design investment may not be immediately apparent and may take years to materialize. Furthermore, it is challenging to quantify the impact of design on competitive performance in a way that is universally accepted and reliable. If managers perceive design as an opportunity to invest in or as just another expense depends on their mindset and attitude towards design.

The lack of management knowledge on the design side and design knowledge on the management side is another driver of the "perception gap".

As mentioned above, Borja de Mozota (2006) points out that the perceived value of design is heavily influenced by the degree of experience with and attitude towards design and/or management (Tab. 1.). According to that, the potential a person sees in design depends on one's progress on the "learning ladder" of design and one's attitude towards management. *"Design management is defined by what you think of design (vertical axis: the 'learning ladder' of design), and by what you think of management (horizontal axis)"* (Borja de Mozota, 2006: 45). (Tab. 1.)

A study conducted by designaustria (advocacy group for Austrian designers) indicates that the understanding of the concept of design is not conveyed during business education or, if at all, it occurs very late. According to the study, 66.7% of the respondents were first introduced to the concept of design through higher education (college, university, or vocational school). The term "design" was addressed in the fields of advertising and marketing, product management, as well as in subjects such as art education and crafts (Willinger and Filek, 2013).

The study further demonstrates a discrepancy between "intentions and actions" on the entrepreneurial side regarding the use of design. According to the findings, 86% of the respondents believe that the implementation of (more) design could provide the economy with greater or new impulses. However, at the same time, 43% of the respondents indicated that they do not employ a designer (either as an employee or freelancer) for their company. (Willinger and Filek, 2013)

Willinger (2015) also found out that 8% of designers in Austria are self-taught and have neither had a vocational nor an academic education.

Gunes (2012) adds that traditional design education is not yet preparing design students for entrepreneurship nor managerial thinking. To him, entrepreneurship is an indispensable condition of design practice, as designers aim to shape the future. Therefore, designers should be educated or at least encouraged on entrepreneurial skills.

Charles Howden and Andrew D. Pressey (2008) name another aspect of the origin of the "perception gap" by referring to "credence goods". These goods are a specific type of product or service where the quality or value is difficult for consumers to assess, even after consumption or use, and which can only be delivered within the framework of a relationship. These relationships are characterized by a high level of information asymmetry, where the seller determines the customer's requirements (e.g. health care and professional services like accountancy or legal services). Unlike tangible goods with easily observable characteristics (such as a car or a smartphone), credence goods have qualities that are not readily verifiable by consumers, requiring them to rely on trust, reputation, or expert advice. In the context of design as a credence good, consumers or clients have limited knowledge or expertise to evaluate the design outcomes accurately. Design is often subjective and involves intangible elements such as aesthetics, user experience, and branding, which may not be immediately measurable or observable by consumers. This places a greater emphasis on the designer's ability to establish trust and to communicate the intended impact and value of their design. Howden and Pressey (2008) note that studies of value creation for credence goods hardly exist.

Murray and Schlacter (1990) add that customers perceive the purchase of a "credence good" as risky because they have difficulties to evaluate their investment even after consumption.

For such goods, price is often seen as an indication of true quality. Hence, there can be a positive rather than negative relationship between price and quantity demanded. Reducing the price of a credence good can undermine

Design as Strategy		
Controling design ROI & business performance and brand value.	Design leadership. Coherence of the design system and driving the future "advanced design".	Design as a resource for the challenges of contemporary managers – Socially responsible enterprise.

Design as Process		
Design research methods – ethno design, etc. Design management as managing the design function.	Integrating design in other processes: brand, innovation, TQM. Design Management as improving the performance of processes.	Integrating design in management decision processes. Design management as inventing the future and "sense building" in a changing environment. Design management for the quality of staff.

Design as Styling		
Integrating design in marketing, R&D, corporate communications. Design management as managing a design project.		

Management as Command & Control	Management as Art of Collective Action	Management as Managing Change

Tab. 1 Design management is defined by what you think of design (Vertical axis: the "learning ladder" of design), and by what you think of management (Horizontal axis). Table after Borja de Mozota (2006)

consumers' assessment of the true quality of the good, leading to less of the good being purchased. (Norman, 2014)

After Bolton (1998), long-time relationships and experience have a positive effect on the customer's benefits derived and the ability to estimate the value created.

II. Four stakeholders and their impact on the "perception gap"

There are four stakeholder groups that are directly affected by and are at the same time able to have a direct influence on the "perception gap": designers, managers (non-designers), design representatives, and business representatives.

Designers are those who create and sell solutions to non-designers. Their challenges regarding the "perception gap" lie in explaining their work and communicating the value they create. These hurdles and efforts to overcome them are widely discussed in literature (Borja de Mozota, 2002, Cross, 2023, Muratovski, 2010, Short, 2011, Cheung, 2012, Cezzar, 2017). The term manager refers to decision makers who use design as a tool to reach a certain goal. Their challenges regarding the "perception gap" are the communication with the designer, tracking of the design process, and justifying an investment in design (Gill, 1990, Micheli et al., 2012, Sebastian, 2005, Chiang et al., 2019, Gill and Graell, 2016, Trueman and Jobber, 1998, Kramoliš and Staňková, 2017).

It is in the interest of both groups to overcome the "perception gap" to smoothen collaboration and foster a superior outcome. The attempts to find a common language, improve the mutual understanding and link design to management frameworks and vice versa is widely discussed in literature (Borja de Mozota, 2006, Landoni et al., 2016, Stevens et al., 2008, Dumas and Mintzberg, 1991, Gorb and Dumas, 1987, Moultrie et al., 2006, Kotler and Alexander Rath, 1984).

Design representatives include design schools, and umbrella associations of the creative industries. Their efforts in shaping the curriculum, demystifying design, and promoting its value are manyfold (Chiang et al., 2019, Brown, 2008, Brown and Katz, 2011). Business representatives include business schools, umbrella associations, and knowledge centers like start-up hubs. There is a lot of literature dealing with the efforts to integrate design in

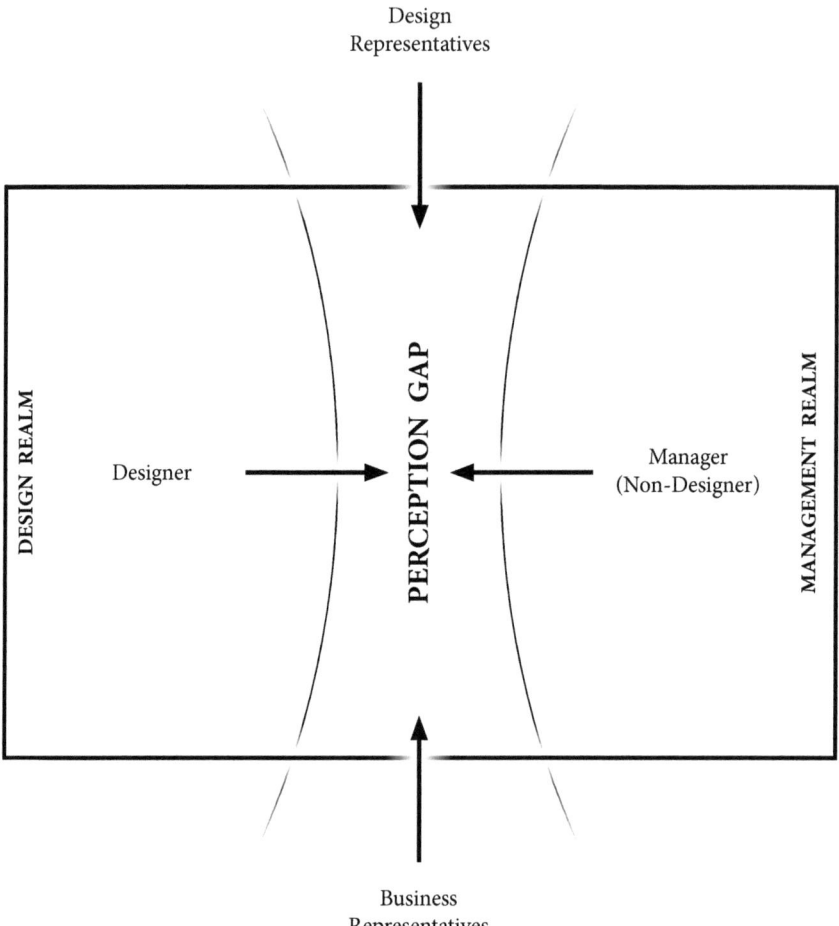

Fig. 2 Visualization of the four stakeholders who have an impact on the "perception gap"
Source: the author, 2023

curricula (Bruder, 2011), make use of the design thinking method (Stevens et al., 2008) and link design to the bottom line (Borja de Mozota, 2006).

Both groups of representatives can have a huge influence on the "perception gap", as they are able to improve the level of knowledge and mutual understanding within the generations to come, and therefore, in the long run.

What is so far hardly covered in literature is a joint effort of these four forces (Fig. 2). What is missing is a common language and an integrated approach over all four areas to improve the status quo and shrink the "perception gap".

Responding to the 'perception gap', there is, for example, a significant need for (graphic) designers to reconsider how they can strengthen or elevate their professional status among the public. In fact, anyone with knowledge of design software is allowed to claim to be a (graphic) designer, including freelancers who work at home, desktop publishing artists who work in printing companies, and so forth. (Chiang et al., 2019)

In Austria, this is mostly because graphic design is a so-called free trade without any obligation to a training or authorization. To change this situation and have a positive and sustainable impact, legislative changes would be needed. This is only possible via a close collaboration of industry representatives and design scholars. (Fig. 2)

CHAPTER THREE

EMPIRICAL PART

To gain deeper insights into the complex relationship between designer and manager (non-designer) and investigate what is needed to improve the mutual understanding, a series of interviews was conducted with eight experts, including designers, managers (non-designers), design representatives, and business representatives.

A. Methodology

The aim of the empirical part is to complete the theoretical findings with the points of view gained from practical experience of the four stakeholders affected by the "perception gap". Following a grounded theory approach (Strauss and Corbin, 1997), conducting semi structured interviews is the most promising approach because it is a qualitative procedure that can be designed very openly and makes follow-up questions possible, if required (Adams, 2015). This allows new aspects to emerge. Likewise, ambiguities can be clarified in person right away.

B. Research Design

I. Survey period

The interviews were conducted after the literature review was written. Because of that, it was possible to design the guiding interview questions (Appendix A, B) in a way that intends to extend and deepen the findings in the literature. The interviews took place in May and June 2023 with an average duration of one hour and sixteen minutes.

IP1	Creative director of a design agency		
	female	duration: 1:14	May 4, 2023
IP2	Founder and creative director of a design agency, university lecturer		
	male	duration: 0:53	May 28, 2023
IP3	Head of marketing at a cultural institution		
	female	duration: 1:37	June 10, 2023
IP4	Entrepreneur, former managing director of a media agency		
	female	duration: 1:20	May 2, 2023
IP5	Director of an advocacy group for designers, university lecturer		
	male	duration: 0:50	May 11, 2023
IP6	University lecturer in higher design education and design represenative at the respective university		
	male	duration: 1:15	May 11, 2023
IP7	High-ranking business representative, entrepreneur		
	male	duration: 1:27	May 12, 2023
IP8	High-ranking representative of higher professional business education, university lecturer		
	female	duration: 1:36	May 9, 2023

Tab. 2 Overview of interview partners (IP 1 – 8)

II. Survey approach

Two interviews were conducted online via MS-Teams. Six interviews were conducted in person. With the consent of the interview partners the interviews were recorded with MS Teams or a voice recorder.

III. Selection criteria for the interview partners

The selection of the interview partners (Tab. 2) was based on Kaiser (2021) and Meuser et. al. (2009). Designers and managers (non-designers) were selected according to Kaiser (2021), for whom experts are considered knowledgeable in a particular field and are identified based on their specific knowledge, position in the community, or their status. Design representatives and business representatives were selected according to Meuser et. al. (2009), who define an expert as someone responsible for the development, implementation, or in control of a solution. Further, they can have privileged access to people or decision making processes.

IV. Guiding interview questions

The guiding interview questions for designers and managers (non-designers) consist of ten structured questions, those for representatives of seven questions (Appendix A, B). The interview questions are directly related to the research questions. Firstly, the experts were asked to provide their perspectives on how designers and managers perceive each other. Understanding these perceptions helps identify potential barriers to effective collaboration. Secondly, the aim was to identify areas of common ground and discrepancies in communication between designers and managers. By uncovering moments of frustration, the interviews aimed to shed light on the underlying causes of the perception gap. Thirdly, the experts provided insights into individual approaches that can bridge the gap. Lastly, the expectations of the four stakeholders towards each other were examined. As recommended by Gläser and Laudel (2010), the interview questions were adapted for each type of expert. They all received similar questions but formulated towards their point of view and according to their field of expertise. Each interview ended with a "Quick win". A spontaneous recap and proposal of an ad-hoc solution by each interview partner.

CHAPTER FOUR

RESULTS AS AGGREGATED FEEDBACK

In the following, the results of eight expert interviews will be summarized as aggregated feedback. Parts of the interviews were shortened or paraphrased. Highly representative statements were quoted. Having the previously mentioned four-forces-perspective in mind, all areas of investigation will be answered from the point of view of all four stakeholder groups.

A. Perspectives on the relationship between designer and manager (non-designer)

To assess the mutual perception, designers, managers, and their representatives first described the relationship between designer and manager from their own experience or observation. In a second step, they were asked to describe in their own words how design could contribute value to a business.

Designers view the relationship with managers as something that can be influenced by themselves a lot, depending on their skills to present themselves, to speak about their work and expertise, and to communicate what can be expected of them and what cannot. (IP2) In the beginning of a cooperation it is important to frame how design can be helpful to shape the right expectations on the client side. It is crucial that the manager understands that a design is not an order they can place, but a cooperative process. *"Working with design is not a one-way road or made-to-order service."* (IP2) *"Managers have to participate in the process to get a good result at the end. They do not have to do a lot but provide the right information for the designer to understand the business at hand."* (IP1) Besides that, designers stated not to have the feeling of being understood in an early stage of a collaboration. Only after the first rounds of explanations. (IP1)

To managers the relationship varies with the background of the business. There is a close collaboration with designers at consumer driven brands, where you could tangibly see the impact of design on the top and bottom line. *"There is a correlation between the role of marketing as a critical function and the appreciation of design. The less marketing and marketing tools are perceived as a critical function, the more design becomes a procurement driven decision based on price more than anything else. Consequently, we have to deal with a lack of understanding and appreciation of design."* (IP4)

SMEs are described as a special category by themselves. SME owners (people who start or inherit a business) are not necessarily marketers or build the business with the customer in mind. *"In my opinion there is the biggest gap, because they do not understand how critical design is in terms of value perception. Maybe to them design is just a cost and not something that drives business. But what I have experienced in my career is that it is much more interesting to work for SMEs because here you can build a brand from scratch and really help them out a lot."* (IP4)

Regarding the relationship to designers, managers stated to not enjoy their roles as cost cutters but are often confronted with financial constraints. *"Currently, we always have to restrict designers because it comes down to a matter of money. [...] When constantly forced to maximize results with a minimal budget, it leads to frustration on both sides, and a lot of design quality and potential is left behind. The designer is not to blame for this, as they can only work with the budget they are given."* (IP3)

First, representatives describe the relationship between designer and manager as a give-and-take one: *"In general, it's about creative freedom versus predefined constraints. This is a matter of trust."* (IP5). They further argue that it would be incorrect to think that these domains are clearly defined and able to meet in the middle of a straight line. (IP6) They report that the most successful collaborations are long-term ones, where designers and managers have gotten to know each other over time and therefore trust each other. *"This is a matter of trust. And success. When the entrepreneur sees economic success, they will give the designer more freedom, and vice versa. If the designer achieves success, they will have greater trust in the company."* (IP5)

Second, they describe it as highly emotional, as design is often judged by its visual surface, but not by the expertise and effort that lies beneath it. The judgment based on personal taste means the relationship can lead to conflicts in the cooperation. (IP8)

"We need to differentiate between two decision-making structures: owner-managed companies, where the decision rests with one person, and corporations with a marketing structure. Both usually have no understanding of advertising, design, ideas, creativity, etc. However, owner-managed companies often have good instincts, a shrewdness combined with intuition. They are usually more willing to take risks because it's their own company, and they don't have to justify themselves to others." (IP7)

At corporations with a marketing structure managers need to justify their decisions to controlling departments or boards. Representatives reported that the difficulty to (immediately) measure the value of design further complicated the relationship between designer and manager. (IP7)

B. Perspectives on the ability of design to contribute value to a business

Designers mentioned two major areas of value contribution. First, they attribute the ability to boost and fuel an entrepreneurial vision or strategic business goal to design. As a strategic tool, design is perceived as interwoven with business decisions (distribution, human resources management, etc.) and as hard to detach from day-to-day operations. Designers do not describe a specific contribution design can make; they refer to the value the design process creates as a whole. (IP2)

"By working with design, a manager will reach a business goal quicker than by not working with design." Designers argue that with a relatively small investment compared to the total spending, the revenue can be increased by a lot. *"The problem is, managers often don't see this connection and designers often don't demonstrate it."* (IP1)

Second, designers point out that through design a company will truly understand the needs of the target group and can therefore improve how they interact and communicate. Asked about the measurability of design, experts reported that this is one of the trickiest aspects. In some cases they can measure it with pre-defined KPIs (# products sold, # clicks on the website, etc.) but most of the time the true value design creates lies in the intangibles (improved image, shift in perception, better communication, etc.). They made the observation that once managers experienced the power of design, they understood it, were convinced, and continued to work with design.

From the designers' perspective, the best way to demonstrate the value of design is within a hands-on project where managers can partly measure and partly sense the values of design. (IP2)

It was reported that clients are easily impressed by winning awards. Designers observed that the less the client knows about design, the more relevant awards become when they decide with whom to collaborate. For designers, awards work only partly as a seal of quality. It is a lot of work to submit a project, sometimes high submission fees occur, and the independence of the jury might be questioned. (IP2)

Nevertheless, designers and agencies participate to compete in search for self-affirmation and public exposure.

Managers described design as a tremendous way to differentiate. To them it creates value by aligning the perception of a brand with the image it tries to conceive. *"Without a proper design, even if you're 100% aligned on your customer promise (experience + product), it doesn't fly because customers are visual beings. And consistency is key."* (IP4) Depending on the manager's experience with design, they see an important moment of added value when designers do not only execute the client's will but come up with solutions they were not asked for. Therefore, it can be assumed that only experienced managers can appreciate the Creative Director as a consultant. (IP4)

Managers find it very difficult to measure the value contribution of design and mentioned three examples: advertising, e-commerce (UI/UX), and brand perception. *"In advertising you can do the modeling: put all other elements of the marketing mix on the same level and only change the creative and you will basically see the difference."* (IP4) *"For example, if after the redesign of a website – the customer journey is more intuitive, it looks more appealing, it's more clear – we're selling 30% more but didn't do anything else but listen to some smart people, that is a very tangible result. In a case like this it would even be fair to give a percentage of revenue increase to the design team."* (IP4) It was proposed to measure the shift in brand perception with a brand tracker but also mentioned that this became harder to track over the last 20 years. *"Two decades ago you had more or less TV, print and the creative. But today everything is much more connected, and the way a brand acts has become more important. That makes it harder to judge design as an isolated parameter."* (IP4)

Managers agreed that although some tools to partly track or measure design exist, there are hardly any clients who are willing to invest in any kind of survey or research on top. One manager talked about an "indirect" way to evaluate the success of design: *"The impact of design is not measured in any form in our case. The lack of time and resources prevents us from doing so. We are just glad if we manage to have a follow-up discussion when things haven't worked out. What we do pay attention to is feedback from external sources, such as voices from the immediate professional or personal environment of decision-makers."* (IP3) When asked if design awards were considered as important, managers responded in two ways: One position pointed out that awards are only relevant for those who know little about design and how the awards are won (IP4). Another manager reported that it is a kind of confirmation for the outcome of a collaboration if a designer wins an award, but that the company is not willing to pay for submissions (IP3).

Business representatives described the value design delivers as communicating and visualizing the values of a business, fostering consistency, and strengthening the recognition value across all media. Some design representatives echoed the description of the managers. Others had a more specific view and described design as an extremely valuable partner to the industry, provided that the industry truly understands the value proposition of design, not merely as the final shaping of a completed process, but as a partner from the very beginning, even in the thought process before any manifestations occur. *"Whenever one honestly, thoroughly, and substantively questions things, interesting results emerge. In my opinion, these results also hold greater long-term value and are not just a quick fix for some immediate, perhaps urgent, need one may have."* (IP6) It was assumed that intensifying this collaboration would be much more interesting and valuable for both sides. *"Design is about systemic thinking, gaining deeper insights and engaging in a process-oriented approach that delivers results that are not purely defined by taste or driven by short-term thinking. So that it represents a service that has deeper value."* (IP6)

Representatives agreed that *"the most pressing question is, how to evaluate design. Business education might tackle the fields of advertisement and online marketing, but not the field of design. Therefore, the evaluation of design or a design agency and the value of design is limited to an emotional, subjective, and very personal level."* (IP8)

C. Perspectives on the pain points in the cooperation between designer and manager (non-designer)

To assess areas of mutual- or misunderstanding, designers, managers, and their representatives were asked to describe the pain points in the cooperation from their own experience or observation. As a second step, they were asked to sketch the ideal designer-manager relationship in their own words.

Designers complained that managers constantly undervalue design, because they have a false perception of the amount of time a designer invests into a project. It was added that this gets worse the more the manager perceives the value of design in relation to the number of items on an order list, instead of having the outcome of the design process in mind. *"It is not the applications that generate the value but the whole process does."* (IP2)

It was assumed that the reason for this might be design's apparent standing as being easily accessible. *"People think because they are able to see it, they are able to judge it. But that is totally wrong".* (IP1)

Designers experience reoccurring discrepancies in the briefing. For them it is difficult if a non-designer sets up the briefing. *"If the designer is not expected to question the briefing and write a re-briefing to identify the real problem before starting to develop a solution, there is a clear misperception of the role of the designer. It gets tricky if the designer is not seen as a sparring partner at eye level but is expected to fulfill a preset."* (IP1) Designers described managers as being overwhelmed by the scope of the design process. Asked for the underlying reason, it was assumed that managers have wrong expectations towards the design process. They expect it to be linear and pre-defined, but it runs in constant loops and transformations, as a dynamic, sometimes even open-ended process. (IP2) Designers complain about a loss of quality if non-designers approve an ambitious concept in the first place but constantly downgrade it later because of internal uncertainty. *"If you want to make a bold design approach you have to be consistent throughout the whole development phase. What managers do not get, is that they cannot pre-assess the success of a new design approach by e. g., focus group interviews. A focus group can only draw references to the things they already know and is not able to give feedback on things they have not seen so far."* (IP1) Furthermore, they describe feedback situations as very frustrating. *"The worst thing is feedback on the level of personal taste. This is just unqualified feedback."* Designers link the bad feedback skills of managers to the general lack of design education in Austria, starting with the misappreciation of design objects and spanning to the misperception of the design profession. *"I do not expect a lot of knowledge on design. People know that a healthy nutrition is good for them. But not even this minimal depth of knowledge is available when it comes to design."* (IP1)

Designers regret that managers often underestimate the phase of implementation. By not providing adequate resources, a lot of potential and value is left on the table. *"We inform and remind the client about the resources needed to implement a design very early in the process. But often this is completely underestimated by the manager and a lot of value is lost in the implementation phase".* (IP1)

Managers get frustrated if a designer always rethinks the briefing: *"As a client I know what I want and I express it clearly. There are projects that offer ample room for visionary thinking and creative freedom. In these cases, there is a great willingness to engage in an exciting collaborative process. However, there are also projects where the focus is on meeting the scope of the brief with high quality under tight time constraints. These fundamental conditions need to be clear to all parties involved. The first scenario allows for multiple iterations and loops, while the second one aims to minimize unnecessary friction. It is the responsibility of the client to choose the right designers for the job, and it is the responsibility of the designer to understand and accept these basic requirements."* (IP3) Managers observed that colleagues with less experience with design often do not have the confidence to decide. To back up their opinion, they start to crowdsource feedback from people they trust like their wife, friends, etc. *"This happens even with top managers, and they are not ashamed to tell you that their wife said it would be better to […] This is where a lot of frustration comes from. As a designer you are now not only pitching to one non-designer, but that person and all their social contacts".* Interview experts proposed to do a focus group interview with people from the relevant target group instead. (IP4) Managers criticize the pricing management of designers as untransparent: *"It is always problematic when a price-offer is not proportional to the scope of the service provided. Especially when a 50% discount is offered right away when asked about cost reduction. It gives the impression that some designers overestimate their value at one moment and then give away a part of their work for free in the next one."*

Design representatives draw attention to the fact that the designer is not a conventional service provider, as design is not about doing what other people already know they want. It was observed that designers and managers often talk past each other, because they speak two completely different languages. As a result, the manager doesn't feel understood, and the creative person doesn't feel their work is sufficiently appreciated. (IP5)

Design representatives also point out that the design process often becomes a big battlefield of pain points that only become visible because of the design process. Especially when brought into the project late, the questions raised can unintentionally turn the design process into a proxy battlefield of divergent future visions within the company. *"This is one of the worst situations designers can find themselves in because they feel powerless, and the outcome is usually unsatisfying."* (IP6)

Experts see another problem in the lack of evidence and the education of designers. *"You don't really have two attempts, one with design and one without. Instead, you only have that one chance. There is insufficient funding available in Austria to provide evidence for the value of design on a broader level. One out of various reasons is a lack of priority, which leads to a lack of initiative. Additionally, the fact that graphic design is an unregulated profession further complicates matters. We have a high percentage, up to 8%, of self-taught individuals in this field. If a project is handled in a less than professional manner, it reflects poorly on the design industry, and companies can be disappointed as a result."* (IP5) In addition, design representatives see a significant lack of knowledge on the manager side on how to select the right partners from the creative industry.

It is concluded by the experts that the gap in perception is underpinned by a fundamental cultural problem. *"In our educational upbringing, we lack interconnected, systemic thinking. We always strive to achieve what is expected of us with as few errors as possible, without considering the bigger picture. If we truly valued having a different kind of culture, we would need to start very early."* (IP6)

Business representatives suspect unawareness on both sides. Managers intervene in the competences of designers by thinking they can judge design on its visual surface. And designers intervene in the domain of the manager by demanding involvement in all kinds of business processes without proper knowledge. *"Both parties want to influence the other one's decision without having a clear picture of the opposite's expertise."* (IP8) They described another friction point that is rooted in fear. *"In hierarchical structures, managers try to anticipate what their superiors might want. To avoid making mistakes they reproduce what already exists, but reproduction is never creative. This friction point is the root of a major misunderstanding because managers want* more of the same *just to be on the safe side, while designers want to break away from the* more of the same.*"* (IP7) Experts link this phenomenon to the lack of education and a lack of role models on the manager as well as on the design side.

D. Perspectives on how an ideal designer-manager-relationship could look like

Designers describe the ideal relationship as *"a collaborative process with a common language and common tools. A process where different expertise and perspectives inspire each other. A process at eye-level with respect and appreciation of each other. A process where the roles of the participants are clear and pre-defined."* (IP2)

Designers see the responsibility to guide through the design process on their territory. *"It is important that the designer leads the path through the project and not the client. With the one exception, if the manager has a lot of experience in branding and the steps suggested are reasonable. But this is hardly the case. We always want to keep it cooperative, but we take the lead. We are even resistant if it is needed."* (IP1)

Managers would appreciate it if the designer brought in a management perspective or at least some kind of understanding. To discuss design decisions not only from a visual but also from a business perspective and in a competitive context. (IP4)

Representatives call design a trust business in two ways: *"Trust in oneself, in one's taste and decisions. And trust in the person I want to work with."* (IP6) According to them, design works best if the decision-making power lies within one single person. Tensions occur if the person in charge is not on the top of the hierarchy, because those people were observed to be driven rather by fear than a personal vision. (IP6)

Business representatives add that the ideal relationship builds on an open mindset with a curiosity to learn from the context of the opposite. It is noted that learning on the job, instead of being prepared by a proper education, leads to a lot of friction and loss of quality during the actual working process. One expert adds: *"It might be easier to make the designer educate the manager than asking the manager to educate themselves. The designers must establish themselves as trustful partners in the eye of the manager and could ideally provide criteria for value evaluation."* (IP8)

E. Perspectives on ways to overcome the "perception gap"

To assess perspectives on how to shrink the "perception gap", designers, managers, and their representatives were asked to describe, in their opinion, what would be needed to improve the mutual understanding.

Designers indicated that a common language would be vital for the improvement of the mutual understanding between designers and managers. (IP2)

"90% of my work is dominated by psychology. I adapt to every single client individually in tone of voice, language, and project structure. If the client is relaxed and calm, I manage the project in these ways. If the client is enthusiastic about tables and numbers I adapt to this need and try to be super precise and correct to win his confidence. Design is very human, highly emotional, unpredictable and artistic as well ... even though it is a business project." (IP1)

It is also seen as a crucial factor to teach Design Management to design students: *"If designers were provided with a skill set in process management and a basic understanding of the management field, this would lead to a new self-perception of the designer and reshape the general perception of the design profession in the long run."* (IP2)

Experts noted that designers need more business knowledge for two reasons:

1. To be perceived as sparring partners at eye level. Especially when it comes to branding, the design task is always connected to the target group, competition, and the market.
2. To become more professional in running their own businesses in a sustainable way. *"Too many designers work for clients for too little money because they just enjoy their design profession. Even if you love what you do, you may not want to give away labor for free. This behavior is very harmful for the whole industry because it lowers the perceived value of design and the monetary value of the design work. Clients own the money needed anyways, they just don't have the respect and appreciation for design to provide a proper budget."* (IP1)

Lastly, designers wished for a better award-culture *"If the short-list in the run-up to the award-ceremony is better called a long-list and awards are used inflationary, there is no sense behind it anymore."* (IP1) and for more budget for the design process *"More budget means more time. This will automatically increase quality."* (IP2)

Managers sense a lack of education on both sides. Managers need to understand the value of design and designers need to understand how to sell the value of their work. They would find it helpful to have more case studies on design that show the problem formulation and path of the design process. *"Making use of good storytelling to explain the process to non-designers in their respective language. Demonstrating tangible value with KPIs and intangible values with a compelling vision."* (IP4)

Managers suggest that a performance-based pricing element could uplift the pricing strategy of designers. On the one hand, they could demonstrate confidence in their own skills and commitment to the result and, on the other hand, they could indicate to be ready to share a part of the risk the manager perceives.

Design representatives are convinced that designers and managers would benefit from an overlap in education. *"Designers would benefit from studying entrepreneurship and learning, and this is actually a problem, that a company is not necessarily an evil entity. That innovation can happen here, which is not necessarily driven by greed."* (IP6) On the other hand, managers would learn not to perceive the world as a fixed outcome. *"Most of the time managers think backwards from where they believe they want to go. And that is the wrong way of thinking. We should think more systemically and consider which positions are helpful in a team to obtain a more holistic view of a problem. From there, we can have a more open perspective on the results based on these complementary competencies."* (IP6) Design representatives see a big need for improvement in design education. *"Many creativity techniques and software programs are taught, but students don't know how to write a proposal or how to strategically position themselves in the market. We have been advocating for this for many years, and while there is some understanding, it seems that there is a lack of time and resources to bring about changes."* (IP5)

Experts encourage designers to work on themselves, by allowing the possibility that non-designers can have good ideas as well. *"It is a sign of personal maturity to learn not to take rejection personally, but rather to analyze it in a way that holds value. After all, even clients can have good ideas. This is part of good collaboration, where one acknowledges that some of the expertise believed to be exclusively one's own can also be attributed to others."* (IP6)

Business representatives argue that managers become more and more the managers of their external business connection to the creative industry. *"They have a lot of supplies at hand, but nobody teaches them how to evaluate, choose, and manage these relationships. Many managers learned on the job how to cooperate with an advertising agency, but nobody thought about how to cooperate with a designer."* (IP8)

Collaborations of business and design universities on Bachelor and Master level could foster a deeper understanding of each other's profession. *"For example, to introduce designers to the process of product development and innovation in a business context and at the same time introduce managers to the design process and the role of the designer. Right now, both disciplines operate as separated silos. Design flies below the radar of managers, society in general and everybody who has the money to pay for it. What is needed is education and a boost for design awareness."* (IP8)

Experts further request the creative industry to be honest with itself regarding awards and ask big agencies to stop creating submission works. Small agencies or individual designers cannot afford to create those and participate with real works, which inherently creates an unfair comparison and a distorted picture. *"If large agencies create submission works at their own expense, it is detrimental to the creative industry. Producing for free seriously questions the value of the delivered work. It also undermines the value of design or a good idea. After all, what is being awarded has never actually been sold to a client."* (IP7)

Business representatives advocate for a consistent wording in proposals and invoices. *"Currently, everyone names the same service differently. That contributes to the perception of design as an untransparent domain."* (IP7)

F. Expectations of designers and managers (non-designers) towards representatives

To assess what is expected from design and business representatives, designers and managers were asked to describe their most urgent demands.

First, designers questioned if their representatives themselves appreciate and recognize the value of design and the impact generated through that work. *"Representatives should have more bite and focus on the things designers really lack. Right now, the wrong people set the wrong priorities."* (IP1)

Second, they demanded that design should no longer be treated as an island. *"Design is interconnected with many other industries. Representatives should foster a livelier exchange spanning various industries, to make design more visible and bring the topic on others' agendas."* (IP2)

Designers argued that these two shifts would change a lot and positive consequences would follow. *"We need a new perspective on the design profession. A professional, business oriented one that is enjoyable, even artistic, but profitable at the same time. A perspective of design as a craft that adds value to society in general. This would change how the mainstream perceives design and improve the way managers work with designers."* (IP1) In this context, designers made a self-critical note and invited fellow designers not to accept the passive role of the victim, as designers who take their profession and industry seriously were representatives themselves. *"The crowd has the ability to replace the institution. Institutions are often rigid and inflexible in their role and function. The design community itself has the potential to be a strong institution and opinion leader."* (IP2) They further expected their industry representatives to set up an official job description for designers. *"This does not exist now in Austria, as design studios have to register and operate as advertising agencies. The concept of design needs to be ideologically broadened and redefined so that it is perceived not only as a visual component but also as a process-oriented and strategic approach. As is already the case in architecture or product design, these fields are already perceived as distinct, complex areas of expertise."* (IP2)

Designers saw an urgent need to integrate design management to the curriculum of design students. They repeated the reasons already mentioned above: 1) To be perceived as sparring partners at eye level. 2) To get more professional in running their own businesses.

Managers demanded their representatives to empower the cooperation of designers and SMEs, as they see potential for both stakeholders in this exchange. SMEs need design but are not aware of that topic and have difficulties to finance a design process. Designers would find a decision-making structure that fits well with the design process. First, experts proposed that a combined funding-and-education program could bring these two groups together and give design a higher priority in the SME context. Second, they argued that a performance based pricing strategy would allow designers to work for less money in the beginning and receive a performance-based bonus after a pre-defined period of time. (IP4) Managers further urged business schools and universities to introduce managers to the value of design and the value of having a creative director as a sparring partner. *"You do not get in touch with design in any education. Even in Marketing and Sales MBAs you touch the topic of design only on the surface. Especially the decision-makers of tomorrow should learn how to judge a creative idea and how to choose the right partner in the first place".* They also demanded design schools and universities to introduce designers to management basics and teach them how to sell and show the value of their work. *"It requires designers to acknowledge their own value, switch from a supplier- to a seller-mode and actively demand fair payment."* (IP4) Experts added that design education must acknowledge that the curriculum must go beyond the aesthetic and conceptual aspects of design and should integrate business-related issues: *"It would be desirable to have more practical projects. Not only on the creative level but also on the business level. Just like it is in real-life after graduation, with everything that comes with it, such as client meetings, feedback, budget constraints, production management, and so on."* (IP3)

Asked if management was part of the designer's education or design was part of the manager's education, designers and managers denied. Experts reported that knowledge was gained on the job, by self-education or acquired from colleagues.

G. Expectations of representatives towards each other or a third-party

Design representatives and business representatives were asked about their needs and what they expect from each other.

Representatives from university business education argued that to make a shift in education some kind of pressure is needed. This pressure could come externally from creative industry representatives and business representatives who could establish a need for a design-trained type of manager. This could result in the educational task to raise design awareness among managers or executives to come. The hypothesis was pushed further by the assumption that a certain amount of pressure from the industry could motivate the ministry of education to fund exchange programs between business and design education. (IP8)

Or it could come internally from an individual teaching at the university with the ambition to run a pilot project. *"The question is in both cases, what could be the underlying motivation to build up that pressure? Does a teacher at a business university see any value in doing a pilot project of collaborating with a design university? If it is successful and companies line up to join the program and students are hired because of that, more programs like that will follow. But the question is if somebody will be able to anticipate that value and start an initiative."* Business representatives stated that the task of introducing managers to design should not solely rely on the designer as an individual but be undertaken by their representative bodies in a broader initiative. *"Managers must justify their spending and it is the duty of the design representatives to attribute value to this spending. Designers must stop demonstrating their value to each other, but start demonstrating it to non-designers"* (IP8)

Design representatives invited business representatives to expand their thinking from the short-term to the long-term as short business cycles make it partly impossible to facilitate in-depth processes. *"Thinking, reflecting, analyzing slows things down. In the current system, this can even be detrimental. A mindset-change is needed to benefit from design solutions that may not deliver immediate results in three months, but perhaps in a year and then continue to grow over the following years."* (IP6) It is assumed that increasing the number of designers on the executive level would have a very positive effect on many companies. *"At Apple, Steve Jobs allowed Johnny Ive, as the Chief Designer, to have an exceptional position compared to other companies. In this constellation, they created value that is not about giving people something they already know they want but something that is so closely connected to people that these products are now deemed essential in their lives. This successful example has existed for years, yet so few companies have learned from it."* (IP6) Some design representatives previously demanded holistic thinking, they also demand holistic action and would prefer to completely rethink school from the ground up as this is assumed to be one of the biggest cultural factors. (IP6) It was added that decisions on education have to be made or at least backed up by policymakers. *"Here, we are back to the question of understanding the role of design. Where does the designer fit from the policymaker's view? Are they perceived as decorators or as an essential part of societal development?"* (IP5)

Others demanded policymakers to approve the introduction of a monetary minimum value for design services and advocated for a minimum fee of 120 euro per hour, as money was at least some form of appreciation. It was argued that this would protect the industry against undervaluation in two ways: 1) against managers who undervalue the work of the designer and try to cut budgets 2) against the recurring problem of self-undervaluation of designers themselves. It was observed that the average rate of a designer is ranging from 60 to 80 euros. After the deduction of social security and income tax, therefore the income often falls below the minimum wage threshold. (IP7)

The summarized findings are added to the visualization of the four stakeholders who have an impact on the "perception gap" (Fig. 3). While the numerous and interconnected pain points within the "perception gap" illustrate the complexity of the designer-manager-relationship, a nonexistent flow of information between designers, managers, and their representatives reveals a kind of gridlock situation.

52   CHAPTER FOUR: RESULTS AS AGGREGATED FEEDBACK

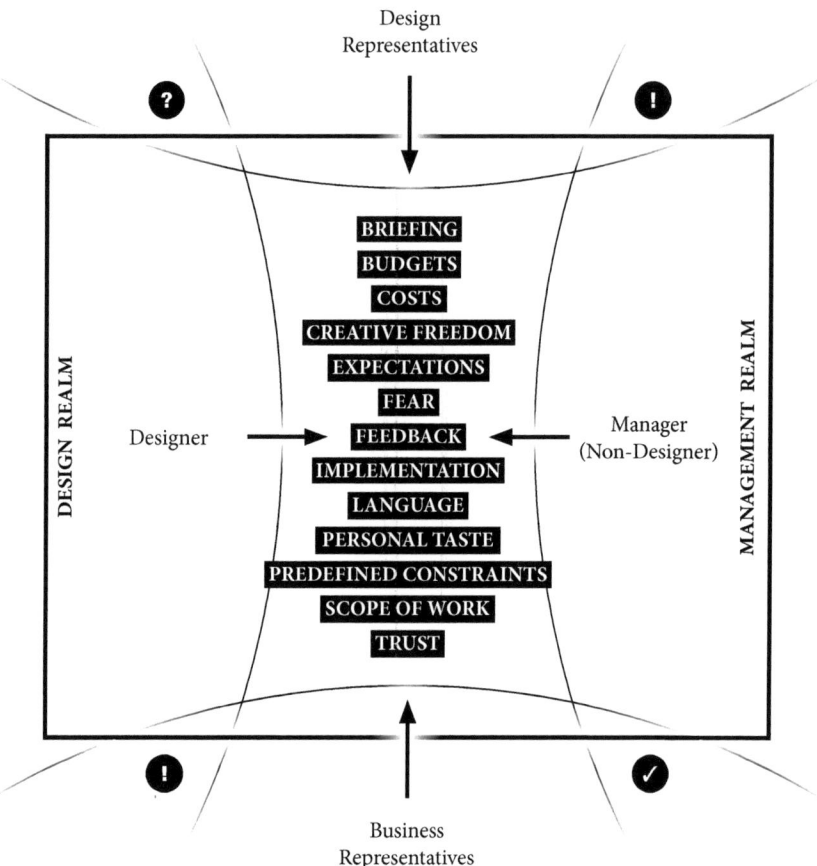

Fig. 3   Findings of the results added to the visualization
of the four stakeholders who have an impact
on the "perception gap"
Source: the author, 2023

CHAPTER FIVE

DISCUSSION AND INTERPRETATION

In this chapter, the research questions are addressed and answered, drawing upon the findings derived from the literature review and the insights obtained from the expert interviews. The integration of these sources allows for a comprehensive analysis of the layers and underlying drivers of the "perception gap".

A. The mutual perception of designers and managers (non-designers)

Effective collaboration between designers and managers (non-designers) plays a crucial role in the success of design projects and organizational operations. However, the literature review and expert interviews showed that a notable "perception gap" exists between these two groups. The first out of four research questions of this thesis …

> Q1: How do designers and managers (non-designers) perceive each other?

… is answered by a critical assessment of the designer-manager-relationship with a focus on the mutual expectations and beliefs regarding design's ability to generate value.

I. The designer-manager-relationship

Experts described the relationship between designers and managers as complex and often driven by misconceptions (IP4) and emotional factors (IP1). Designers acclaimed that they hardly feel understood in the beginning of a relationship. Only after some rounds of explanation and a certain willingness of the manager to listen, common ground can be established. This phenomenon was reflected in literature, where design was described as a domain that is difficult to understand and evaluate (Cross, 2023, Stevens et al., 2008, Lorenz, 1994, Sheppard et al., 2018).

Managers observed a closer relationship with designers at consumer-driven companies than at sales- or operation-driven companies: *"There is a correlation between the role of marketing as a critical function and the appreciation of design. The less marketing and marketing tools are perceived as a critical function, the more design becomes a procurement-driven decision based on price more than anything else. Consequently, we have to deal with a lack of understanding and appreciation of design."* (IP4)

The expert interviews further revealed that the relationship also varies with how a business is structured and decisions in the design process are made. The fewer people are involved in decision-making, the smoother the relationship seems to be.

Experts agreed with Bolton (1998) that experience plays a vital role in fostering a successful designer-manager-relationship. Long-term collaborations built on trust and familiarity tend to yield better outcomes: *"In general, it's about creative freedom versus predefined constraints. This is a matter of trust"* (IP5). As the entrepreneur sees economic success, they become more willing to provide the designer with more freedom, and vice versa.

II. The power of design

As the relationship between designer and manager varies by business context, professional background, and degree of experience, so do the beliefs of and expectations towards design to contribute value to a business. Borja de Mozota (2006) identified the combination of the progress on the "learning ladder" of design and the beliefs of management as an enabling or inhibiting driver in this context (Tab. 1.).

Designers said that they create value by not doing what other people already know they want. *"Whenever one honestly, thoroughly, and substantively questions things, interesting results emerge. In my opinion, these results also hold greater long-term value and are not just a quick fix for some immediate, perhaps urgent, need one may have"* (IP6). They described design as a process that is interwoven with day-to-day business decisions and found it hard to detach those things from another. Therefore, designers do not speak of the one specific value contribution design can make, but the value the whole process creates (IP2).

Literature agreed by attributing design with the ability to boost and fuel an entrepreneurial vision or strategic business goal. Stevens et al. (2008) and Borja de Mozota (2006) referred to Porter's Generic Strategies Framework (Porter, 1996), Porter's Five Forces (Porter, 1985) and Porter's Value Chain. They highlighted design's power to strengthen a company's general position on the market (*differentiation, cost leadership, focus*), to manipulate external forces (the threat of new entrants, the bargaining power of suppliers, the bargaining power of buyers, the threat of substitute products or services, and the intensity of rivalry among existing competitors), and to fuel primary operations (inbound logistics, operations, outbound logistics, marketing and sales, service).

Most of the managers recognized design in one out of three of Porter's Generic Strategies – *differentiation*. They described design as a *"tremendous way to differentiate"* (IP4), and a way to align the perception of a brand with the image it tries to conceive: *"Without a proper design, even if you're 100% aligned on your customer promise (experience + product), it doesn't fly because customers are visual beings. And consistency is key"* (IP4). Only managers who had experience with working with design mentioned it to *focus* on new market segments. They didn't mention it in connection with a *cost-leadership* position. Stevens et al. (2008) referred to Moultrie et al. (2006) who found that this function of design is hardly recognized, as in a company that aims for minimizing all costs, design might be seen as an unnecessary expense.

It can be concluded that managers in general underestimate the power of design. This hinders them to use design to their full advantage, because they are not aware of many of the benefits it could provide to them as was mentioned by Trueman and Jobber (1998).

When it came to quantifying the value of design, managers have had good experiences with tracking design's tangible impact on e-commerce (UI/UX): *"For example, if after the redesign of a website – the customer journey is more intuitive, it looks more appealing, it's more clear – we're selling 30% more but didn't do anything else but listened to some smart people, that is a very tangible result [...]"* (IP4).

The more intangible the value of design became, the harder it got to pinpoint the exact reason for value creation, as stated by Kramoliš and Staňková (2017), who discussed the difficulty of isolating the impact of design investment from other factors that may affect competitive performance. Landoni (2016) mentioned that, as of today, the dynamics between investment in design and competitive performance were poorly analyzed.

While design professionals seemed to live well with the fact that some aspects of design lie within the intangibles and can only be sensed but not quantified (IP1), hierarchical structures urge managers to justify and proof spending (IP8). Borja de Mozota (2006) proposed to demonstrate the value of design by the economic-value-added (EVA) framework and to capture it with the Balanced Score Card model. The Design Management Institute (DMI, 2013) created the *The Design Value Index* to demonstrate design's long-time value contribution to business performance.

Also, Kotler and Rath (1984) highlighted the difficulties in attributing valuable contributions to either the design or management side. They established the terms *silent design* and *silent design in reverse* and gave a name to what designers previously expressed as *"hard to detach"*.

Interestingly, designers and managers were neither aware of Borja de Mozota's suggestions, nor the existence of *The Design Value Index* nor Kotler and Rath's naming of the value contribution-problem. This is very disadvantageous, as these tools do exist, but are obviously not used in day-to-day work to communicate the value of design or justify investments in design.

B. The key pain points that contribute to the misunderstanding in communication between designers and managers (non-designers)

Literature addressed the following key factors of contributing to the "perception gap" between designers and managers: a lack of a common language and the poor analysis of the dynamics between investment in design and competitive performance (Landoni et al., 2016), the necessity of experience and corresponding expectations (Borja de Mozota, 2006), a lack in education (Willinger and Filek, 2013), and design's hardly explored nature of being a "credence good" that is hard to grasp (Howden and Pressey, 2008, Murray and Schlacter, 1990, Bolton, 1998).

To answer the second research question …

> Q2: *What are the key pain points that contribute to the misunderstanding in communication between designers and managers (non-designers)?*

… the findings from the literature are combined with the following moments of discrepancy/misunderstanding that were reported to occur during the designer-manager collaboration: the briefing, the scope of work, costs, budgets, trust, fear, feedback, personal taste, predefined constraints, creative freedom, and implementation.

I. Briefing for and scope of the design process

A lot of value can be generated or lost as well at an early as at a late phase of a cooperation. Designers reported that sometimes non-designers create briefings and see those as given but mostly the real problem is hidden underneath those assumptions: *"If the designer is not expected to question the briefing and write a re-briefing to identify the real problem before starting to develop a solution, there is a clear conflict and misperception of the role of the designer. It gets tricky if the designer is not seen as a sparring partner at eye level but is expected to fulfill a preset."* (IP6)

On the contrary, managers argued that designers must understand that not every project has the resources and budget to allow for such a stirring process: *"There are those projects that offer ample room for visionary thinking and creative freedom. [...] However, there are also those projects where the focus is on meeting the scope of the brief with high quality under tight time and budget constraints. [...] it is the responsibility of the designer to understand and accept these basic requirements."* (IP3)

These differing expectations towards the scope of the design process can cause misunderstandings and frustrations at the very beginning of a cooperation. Even worse, the questions a holistic design process raises could turn every project meeting into a battlefield for conflicts or divergent future visions.

The implementation of a design solution into the day-to-day business is another hot topic that is directly linked to the perception of the scope of the design process. Designers pointed out that a lot of value is sometimes lost during the implementation phase. *"We inform and remind the client about the resources needed to implement a design very early in the process. But often this is completely underestimated by the manager".* (IP1)

The degree of un-/awareness of the manager is connected to the progress on the "learning ladder" of design. The lower the level of design awareness as shown by Borja de Mozota (2006), the more prone to error the manager's assumption gets.

II. Costs and budgets

Because of the poor analysis of the dynamics between investment in design and competitive performance (Landoni et al., 2016), costs are a hot topic in the designer-manager-relationship.

Designers blamed managers of having a false perception of the amount of time they invest into a solution. They saw two major reasons for that:

1. A lot of the design-work is invisible, because it consists of research, thinking and problem solving. That makes it hard for non-designers to estimate the working hours. Suppositionally a manager is inexperienced with design, this person might not even be aware of the scope of the design process as mentioned above.
2. Design is often seen as the sum of items on an order list, instead of the outcome of the whole design process. *"This leads to an undervaluation of design. […] It is the process that generates the value, not the applications listed."* (IP2)

Managers reported to perceive the pricing of design as untransparent: *"It is always problematic when a price-offer is not proportional to the scope of the service provided. Especially when a 50% discount is offered right away when asked about cost reduction. It gives the impression that some designers overestimate their value at one moment and then give away a part of their work for free in the next one."* (IP3)

Three underlying causes for this appeared during the research for this thesis:

1. As graphic design in Austria is a so-called free trade the qualification can range from university degree to self-taught. It was mentioned by the interview experts and the literature that in Austria 8% of designers are self-taught individuals (IP5 and Willinger, 2015). This range of variation in professionalism further complicates matters, as a manager could get two very different offers for the same project.
2. As Gunes (2012) pointed out, designers are not educated on managerial aspects. The understanding of costs and the development of a consistent pricing strategy relies on the designer's ability to explain the scope of work

or name the invisible elements of the design process. In fact, designers get hardly any training in sales or price management during their education.
3. As design can be characterized as a "credence good" (Howden and Pressey, 2008), the seller determines the customer's requirements. The best solution can be a cheap ad-hoc one or a more expensive holistic one, depending on the type of problem. The client must rely on the seller's expertise to know what's right. In this context it was very hard for the manager to compare two different price-offers.

The size of the budget was described as another friction point by designers and managers alike. Managers reported that they do not enjoy their roles as cost-cutters but are very often confronted with very narrow financial constraints. *"Currently we always have to restrict designers because it always comes down to a matter of money. [...] When constantly forced to maximize results with a minimal budget, it leads to frustration on both sides, and a lot of design quality and potential is left behind. The designer is not to blame for this, as they can only work with the budget they are given."* (IP3). Getting the size of the budget right was described by one interview expert as a balancing act between *"creative freedom versus predefined constraints"* (IP5).

Design representatives sensed a significant lack of knowledge on the manager's side on how to select the right partners from the creative industry (IP5). It can be assumed that if managers would be better informed about the different circumstances and conditions of working with an advertising agency, a design studio, or a freelance Art Director they could better align the selection of the business partner to match their requirements from the very beginning and minimize friction in the process to come.

III. Trust and fear in decision-making

Design's nature of being a "credence good" as described by Howden and Pressey (2008) brings trust and fear as highly emotional factors to the decision-making process. Managers found it hard to make decisions on design because they were not able to analyze and judge the solution at hand as they were used to. Norman (2014) found the reason for this in a high level of information-asymmetry. The fact that the design provided was just one solution out of potentially infinite possibilities added another layer of uncertainty (IP6). Designers were aware of the problem: *"If one is not confident in oneself, it can be incredibly difficult to make a decision"* (IP1). Design representatives described design as a trust business in two ways: *"Trust in oneself, in one's taste and decisions. And trust in the person I want to work with."* (IP6)

Howden and Pressey (2008) agreed and noted that in the context of a "credence good" it requires the client to rely on trust, reputation, or expert advice. This uncertainty is the reason why managers attach importance to feedback from a third party. The urge to confirm their intuition to come to a decision, makes them seek for a proof of quality from sources or people they trust.

Design awards were mentioned and at the same time criticized as a possible seal of quality. On the one hand, they can provide guidance (IP4) or confirmation (IP3) to non-designers. On the other hand, they were perceived as too expensive, inflationary (IP1), or unfair (IP7) by designers and their representatives. From a purely objective point of view, design awards could work as an effective remedy to make design as a "credence good" a bit more tangible to non-designers. To turn this friction point into a win-win-situation, design experts demanded an internal re-thinking of the "award-culture". Splitting the cost of the submission fee between designer and non-designer could take both parties a step closer to this beneficial situation.

Designers also reported that managers crowdsourced for feedback. Instead of seeking expert advice, they asked their wife or friends – people who are neither qualified to judge design nor part of the target group. *"This happens even with top managers, and they are not ashamed to tell you that their wife said it would be better to [...] This is where a lot of frustration comes from. As a designer you are now not only pitching to one non-designer, but that person and all their social contacts".* (IP1)

Designers complained that because of this recurring behavior a lot of unprofessional feedback enters the design process, making it highly emotional, and diluting its quality. To designers, feedback on the level of personal taste was the worst kind of feedback. According to Short (2011), the low and rather generalized perception of design as an aesthetic add-on is responsible for what design representatives have observed: *"To non-designers design seems easily accessible and familiar. Some might think that because they have eyes to look and see, they can judge design, just because it is visual."* (IP6)

To avoid this dilemma, experts from the management realm recommended their colleagues to seek qualified advice or to do a focus group interview with people from the relevant target group if the design should be pre-tested (IP4). Designers hold against that argument and pointed out the following limitations: *"What managers do not get, is that you cannot pre-assess the success of a new design approach by focus group interviews. A focus group can only draw references to the things they already know and is not able to give feedback on things they have not yet seen."* (IP1)

The uncertainty in decision-making fosters a fear-dominated mindset among managers, especially in the context of a hierarchical business structure. *"People are trying to anticipate what their superiors might want. They avoid making mistakes by reproducing what already exists"* (IP6). This fear-driven friction point is the root of a major conflict between manager and designer: One group aims for *more of the same,* to be on the safe side, while the other group aims for *innovation*.

The fear-dominated mindset was also reflected in Murray and Schlacter's comment that the purchase of a "credence good" is perceived as risky (Murray and Schlacter, 1990). To include a performance-based element in a designer's pricing strategy could demonstrate commitment to managers and open new economic perspectives to designers. A positive side effect would be that thanks to this self-assured proposal, managers could sense the perceived risk as a shared one. Unfortunately, from today's perspective, designers lack the economic knowledge to develop or implement such a pricing strategy.

C. Overcoming the "perception gap"

The integration of findings from the literature review and expert interviews offers valuable insights on enhancing mutual understanding between designers and managers. The upcoming paragraphs aim to answer the third research question …

Q3: *How can the "perception gap" be overcome?*

… by synthesizing the perspectives at hand to identify key requirements for improving collaboration and communication between the two parties.

I. Common language and values

Interviewed experts of all four stakeholder groups mentioned that they often talked past each other. *"And as a result, managers don't feel understood, and designers don't feel like their work is sufficiently appreciated."* (IP5) The necessity of a common language between design and management was also a recurring issue in the literature (Gill, 1990, Micheli et al., 2012, Sebastian, 2005, Chiang et al., 2019, Gill and Graell, 2016).

For a successful cooperation it is crucial that managers do not only speak business language and designers do not only speak design language (Micheli et al., 2012). Designers reported that they try to individually adapt in tone of voice, language, and project structure to every client. The managers' wishes for consistent wording in proposals and invoices further illustrate that need. Representatives reported that *"currently, everyone names the same service differently."* (IP7)

The research for this thesis revealed a very interesting example of designers and management literature talking at cross-purpose. While designers emphasized the importance of perceiving *design as a process* (IP1, IP2, IP6), Borja de Mozota (2006) defined the highest step on the "learning ladder" of design as *design as strategy* (Tab. 1.). *Design as process* is one step below, just above *design as styling*. Obviously, design experts and Borja de Mozota want to express similar thoughts, but do so in a different, even contradictory, way.

II. Getting expectations right

Although both groups may share a common objective, their expectation of how to reach the goal might be very different. A dissonance in expectations was mentioned in connection with the scope and range of services of the designer, the structure of the design process, and design's ability to contribute to value creation. These issues could be tackled by education, with examples of best practice and by mutual learning. Getting the expectations on both sides right from the very beginning of a project would help to find the sweet spot between predefined constraints and creative freedom, smoothen the set-up of a design process and reduce unnecessary friction during the collaboration.

III. Education on both sides

Education is seen as a major factor to shrinking the "perception gap". All interviewed experts, as well as the literature, called the lack of education on the design and the business side an underlying driver of many pain points in the designer-manager-relationship. Especially Borja de Mozota (2006), Willinger and Filek (2013), and Gunes (2012) found a correlation between the level of education and the quality of the relationship.

Designers have a need for more business knowledge for three reasons:

1. To be perceived as sparring partners at eye level by managers.
2. To understand how to sell the value of their work.
3. To get more professional in running their own businesses.

Managers have a need for more knowledge on design to:

1. Understand and communicate the value of design and thereby justify their spending.
2. Select the right partners from the creative industries.
3. Capture the full potential of the value design can provide.

Fostering collaboration across professions is seen as a core issue by representatives, because from collaboration knowledge and awareness will follow. *"Design flies below the radar of managers, society in general and everybody who has the money to pay for it. What is needed is education and a boost for design awareness."* (IP 8)

D. The mutual expectations of designers, managers (non-designers) and representatives

The subsequent discussion highlights the pressing demands expressed by designers and managers towards their representatives. It further delves into the reciprocal expectations between design and business representatives. The last research question …

Q4: *What is expected from representatives?*

… is answered by shedding light on the forces that influence the size of the "perception gap".

I. Designers demand true representation and a re-definition of the design profession

Designers raised doubts about the way they are represented. They did not see the right priorities and wanted design representation to open a broader discussion on design. *"Representatives should foster a livelier exchange spanning various industries, to make design more visible and bring the topic on others' agendas."* (IP1)

Cheung (2012) already noticed the low perception of design as troublesome and underlined the designer's need of *"a new perspective on the design profession."* (IP1) Following Chiang et al. (2019), designers demanded representatives to develop an official definition of running a design business. Now, design studios in Austria can only be run as a so-called unprotected free trade or registered as an advertising agency. The former does not represent their educational background. The latter does not correspond with the scope of their work – even worse – it intensifies the confusion on the difference between advertising and design. At least it provides some protection regarding labor and trade law. Furthermore, they expected industry representatives to elevate the designer's professional status by integrating design management into the curriculum. Gunes (2012) agreed, named entrepreneurship an indispensable condition for design practice and pointed out that designers should be educated or at least encouraged on entrepreneurial skills. *"If designers were provided with a skill set in process management and a basic understanding of the management field, this would lead to a new self-perception of the designer and reshape the general perception of the design profession in the long run."* (IP2)

II. Managers demand access to design for SMEs and an integration of design into business education and vice versa

Managers demanded representatives to make design accessible for SMEs because they saw unused potential in such a cooperation. *"SMEs do not yet understand how critical design is in terms of value perception. To them, design is still a cost and not seen as something that drives business."* (IP4) Three demands to bring SMEs and designers together were raised:

1. The integration of design in existing founder's programs.
2. A funding program to help SMEs in running and financing a design process.
3. A legal framework for a performance-based pricing strategy to lower the entry barrier of SMEs to design and provide an attractive long-term perspective to

designers. This idea was echoed in statements of representatives who also see a positive correlation of the owner-led business structure and a smooth decision-making process.

Furthermore, managers followed Stevens et al. (2008) and Borja de Mozota (2006) by urging business education to introduce managers to the value of design and design education to introduce designers to management basics. Literature pointed at the relation of the ability to utilize design and the level of knowledge on management literature. While the value contribution of design was widely acknowledged in management literature (Borja de Mozota, 2006, Landoni et al., 2016, Stevens et al., 2008, Dumas and Mintzberg, 1991, Gorb and Dumas, 1987, Moultrie et al., 2006, Kotler and Alexander Rath, 1984, Kramoliš and Staňková, 2017), managers still found it hard to engage with design in day-to-day practice.

III. Design representatives demand longer business cycles, and the support of policymakers to completely rethink school from the ground up

Design education representatives demanded business representatives to expand their thinking from the short-term to the long-term. They echoed Trueman and Jobbler (1998) in pointing out that short business cycles limit opportunities for longer, more valuable in-depth design processes: *"Thinking, reflecting, analyzing slows things down. In the current system, this can even be detrimental. It is a systemic problem, a conflict that is difficult to resolve"* (IP 6). They further advocated not only for holistic thinking but holistic action. Gill and Graell (2016) stated that design and management are not only two different disciplines, but they are also two different cultures. Design education representatives agreed: *"I would prefer to completely rethink universities ... preferably to completely rethink school from the ground up. Because it is one of the biggest cultural factors."* (IP 6).

Design industry representatives demanded more design awareness from policymakers, as they need their back-up to facilitate changes like an update of the curriculum or a minimum hourly rate. They saw a major hurdle in the low and generalized perception of the design profession as mentioned by Muratovski (2010) and Short (2011): *"Here, we are back to the question of understanding the role of design. Where does the designer fit from the policymaker's view? Are they perceived as decorators or as an essential part of societal development?"* (IP5).

They affirmed to have been advocating for a bottom-up approach and better alignment – of design education and the skill set designers need to survive on the market – for many years. *"While there is some understanding, it seems that there is a lack of time and resources to bring about changes"* (IP5).

IV. Business representatives demand more pressure to raise design awareness and hold design representatives accountable for doing the same

Business education representatives pointed out that to create a shift in university business education and raise design awareness among managers, external (from the creative industry representatives and business representatives) or internal (from individuals teaching at the university) pressure was needed. To build up the pressure, the current gridlock situation must be overcome and a spark to initiate mutual learning lit.

Furthermore, business representatives hold design representatives accountable for introducing managers to design and added that this task should not solely rely on the designer as an individual but be undertaken in a broader initiative. (IP8)

CHAPTER SIX

CONCLUSION & FUTURE MANAGERIAL IMPLICATIONS

This master's thesis tackles the gap in the perception of the value of design between designers and managers (non-designers) and roots in the observations the author made during more than fifteen years of working as a designer in the creative industries. A review of the existing literature was undertaken and combined with the insights of eight expert interviews to gain deeper insights into the complex relationship between designers and managers (non-designers) and investigate what is needed to improve the mutual understanding.

It was found that the "perception gap" can only be overcome via a redefinition of the design profession, a common language for designers and managers (non-designers), and ways to measure design at least partly. This could be achieved by legislative changes, a shift in design as well as business education, a re-thinking of design-award-culture and breaking up the silos of design and management to initiate a discussion on design across industries. Legislative changes would enable design to establish itself as a stand-alone profession. Not being subordinated to advertising anymore could spark a new perspective on the design profession, for designers themselves but also managers and society in general. A shift in education would be necessary to move the learning experience from on-the-job to education. If managers would learn about design and designers would learn about management, ideally through active collaboration, they would develop an understanding of and empathy for the opposite domain, be able to formulate common objectives, establish a common language, not only in the sense of expectations and values, but also in the sense of vocabulary, and openly talk about risk and risk-sharing.

A re-thinking of the design-award-culture could equip designers with an instrument to demonstrate their value and managers with a guiding seal of quality when searching for a business partner or trying to evaluate the outcome of a collaboration.

Management literature already suggests promising ways to demonstrate and capture the impact design has on a business, but apparently this knowledge is not transferred to daily common practice yet. A change in curriculum could, in the long run, enable this flow of information from theory to practice and therefore create tools to partly measure design available for designers and managers alike.

The research for this thesis revealed that designers, managers, and design and business representatives already made various, but separate, attempts to bridge the "perception gap" without any major progress. What was so far hardly covered, neither in literature nor during the expert interviews, is a joint effort of these four forces to find a solution to get out of this gridlock.

Business representatives asked the legitimate question where the motivation for such an integrated initiative can come from. In the following, the author shares fundamental ideas on how an integrated initiative could be started and provides food for thought to future research. The author assumes that to get all four stakeholders aboard a common vision for the role of design in business context must be established. This could start with designers and design representatives, who must align their future vision of the design profession. This vision must then be translated into business language, so to speak into a tangible economic opportunity, to get the attention of business representatives and executives alike. Only if all four stakeholders are aware of the bigger picture and the economic potential, they will have the motivation to make or support changes in their area of influence and find an open ear for it for the very first time.

A change in education could not be made from one day to another but could be worked at with a combination of a bottom-up approach, to educate the generations to come, and a top down approach, to reach active executives. As school was mentioned as a major influence factor to change culture, this approach is a slow and long-term one and will make collaboration easier for the designers and managers of tomorrow. To improve the situation for those who are actively working, it seems promising to educate the people at the top of the hierarchy and infiltrate organizations from there with a redefined perception of design. In parallel, a channel or format for open communication between designers and managers must be established by themselves or representatives to foster a culture of exchange and mutual learning. This open and frequent dialog will help in finding a common language, not only in the sense of expectations and values (to talk about the same thing), but also in the sense of vocabulary (to literally speak the same language). Even the most basic learning would be beneficial, for instance if managers learn the difference between design and advertising and designers understand the difference between revenue and profit.

By implementing these strategies, designers, managers, design representatives, and business representatives can take advantage of new synergies to bridge the "perception gap" and harness the full potential of design on an economic as well as on a societal level.

LIMITATIONS

It is important to acknowledge the following limitations of this thesis to ensure a balanced understanding of the research findings. 1) The study was limited to eight expert interviews, which may not fully represent the diverse perspectives within the field of designer-manager relationships. The findings should be interpreted with caution and may not be generalizable to the entire population of designers and managers. 2) The data collected in this study relied on self-reported perceptions and experiences of the participants. This method is subject to recall bias and individual interpretation. Participants' responses may be influenced by their own biases or limited understanding of the dynamics between designers and managers. 3) The author of the thesis is a (graphic) designer. This introduces the potential for bias in the interpretation and analysis of the data as the author's background and personal experiences might influence the conclusions drawn from the interviews.

REFERENCES

ADAMS, W. C. 2015. Conducting semi-structured interviews. *Handbook of practical program evaluation,* 492–505.

BENNETT, A. 2011. *ICOGRADA Design Education Manifesto 2011.*

BOLTON, R. N. 1998. A dynamic model of the duration of the customer's relationship with a continuous service provider: The role of satisfaction. *Marketing science,* 17, 45–65.

BORJA DE MOZOTA, B. 2002. Design and competitive edge: A model for design management excellence in European SME's.

BORJA DE MOZOTA, B. 2006. The four powers of design: A value model in design management.

BROWN, T. 2008. Design thinking. *Harvard business review,* 86, 84.

BROWN, T. & KATZ, B. 2011. Change by design. *Journal of product innovation management,* 28, 381–383.

BRUDER, R. 2011. Mutual inspiration and learning between management and design. *The handbook of design management,* 144–160.

CEZZAR, J. 2017. What Is Graphic Design?" aiga| the Professional Association for Design. October, 5, 2017.

CHEUNG, B. 2012. Double'Blind Spots' of the academia and design industry. Hong Kong.

CHIANG, W. S., IDRIS, M. Z. & CHUEN, T. W. 2019. Is graphic design being taken seriously as a profession. *Journal of Arts and Social Sciences,* 3, 1–9.

CROSS, N. 2023. DESIGN THINKING: *Understanding how designers think and work,* Bloomsbury Publishing.

DMI. 2013. *The Value of Design* [Online]. Available: https://www.dmi.org/page/DesignValue [Accessed 28.3.2023].

DUMAS, A. & MINTZBERG, H. 1991. Managing the form, function, and fit of design. *Design Management Journal (Former Series),* 2, 26–31.

GILL, C. & GRAELL, M. Teaching design thinking: Evolution of a teaching collaboration across disciplinary, academic and cultural boundaries. DS 83: Proceedings of the 18th International Conference on Engineering and Product Design Education (E&PDE16), Design Education: Collaboration and Cross-Disciplinarity, Aalborg, Denmark, 8th-9th September 2016, 2016. 034–039.

GILL, H. 1990. Adoption of design science by industry—why so slow? *Journal of Engineering Design*, 1, 289–295.

GLÄSER, J. & LAUDEL, G. 2010. *Experteninterviews und qualitative Inhaltsanalyse*, Springer Verlag.

GORB, P. & DUMAS, A. 1987. Silent design. *Design studies*, 8, 150–156.

GUNES, S. 2012. Design entrepreneurship in product design education. *Procedia-Social and Behavioral Sciences*, 51, 64–68.

HOWDEN, C. & PRESSEY, A. D. 2008. Customer value creation in professional service relationships: the case of credence goods. *The Service Industries Journal*, 28, 789–812.

KAISER, R. 2021. Qualitative Experteninterviews: Konzeptionelle Grundlagen und praktische Durchführung (2., aktualisierte Auflage). *Elemente der Politik*.

KOTLER, P. & ALEXANDER RATH, G. 1984. Design: A powerful but neglected strategic tool. *Journal of business strategy*, 5, 16–21.

KRAMOLIŠ, J. & STAŇKOVÁ, P. 2017. Design and its impact on the financial results of enterprises (based on managers' opinions). *Journal of Competitiveness*.

LANDONI, P., DELL'ERA, C., FERRALORO, G., PERADOTTO, M., KARLSSON, H. & VERGANTI, R. 2016. Design Contribution to the Competitive Performance of SMEs: The Role of Design Innovation Capabilities. *Creativity and Innovation Management*, 25, 484–499.

LORENZ, C. 1994. Harnessing design as a strategic resource. *Long Range Planning*, 27, 73–84.

MEUSER, M. & NAGEL, U. 2009. The expert interview and changes in knowledge production. *Interviewing experts*, 17–42.

MICHELI, P., JAINA, J., GOFFIN, K., LEMKE, F. & VERGANTI, R. 2012. Perceptions of industrial design: The "means" and the "ends". *Journal of Product Innovation Management*, 29, 687–704.

MOULTRIE, J., CLARKSON, P. J. & PROBERT, D. 2006. A tool to evaluate design performance in SMEs. *International Journal of Productivity and Performance Management.*

MURATOVSKI, G. 2010. Design and Design Research: The Conflict between the Principles in Design Education and Practices in Industry. *Design Principles & Practice: An International Journal,* 4.

MURATOVSKI, G. 2021. Research for designers: A guide to methods and practice. *Research for Designers,* 1–100.

MURRAY, K. B. & SCHLACTER, J. L. 1990. The impact of services versus goods on consumers' assessment of perceived risk and variability. *Journal of the Academy of Marketing science,* 18, 51–65.

NORMAN, G. 2014. Credence Good. *Dictionary of Industrial Organization.* Edward Elgar Publishing Limited.

NUSSBAUM, B. 2004. The power of design. *Business week,* 17, 2004.

PAPANEK, V. 2020. Design for the Real World, Ed. 3. Thames & Hudson Ltd, London.

PORTER, M. E. 1985. Technology and competitive advantage. *Journal of business strategy,* 5, 60–78.

PORTER, M. E. 1996. What is strategy?

SEBASTIAN, R. 2005. The interface between design and management. *Design Issues,* 21, 81–93.

SEIDEL, V. P. 2000. Moving from design to strategy: the four roles of design-led strategy consulting. *Design Management Journal,* 11, 35–40.

SHEPPARD, B., YEON, H. & LONDON, S. 2018. Tapping into the business value of design. *The McKinsey Quarterly.*

SHORT, D. 2011. The consummate curriculum for the undergraduate graphic design student in the United States. Savannah College of Art and Design.

STEVENS, J., MOULTRIE, J. & CRILLY, N. 2008. Designing and design thinking in strategy concepts: Frameworks towards an intervention tool.

STRAUSS, A. & CORBIN, J. M. 1997. *Grounded theory in practice,* Sage.

TRUEMAN, M. & JOBBER, D. 1998. Competing through design. *Long range planning,* 31, 594–605.

WILLINGER, U. 2015. Österreichische Designstatistik, Wirtschaftskraft und gesellschaftspolitische Bedeutung.

WILLINGER, U. & FILEK, S. 2013. *Designbewusstsein in Österreichs Unternehmen.*

APPENDIX

A. Guiding interview questions for designers and managers (non-designers)

I	The mutual perception of designers and managers (non-designers)

Q1:	How would you describe the relationship between designers and managers?
→	Was management/design part of your education? How?

Q2:	DESIGNERS: How can design contribute value to a business?
	MANAGERS: How do you expect design to add value to your company?

Q3:	Do you feel understood/respected?

II	The key pain points that contribute to the misunderstanding in communication between designers and managers (non-designers)

Q4:	DESIGNERS: How do you convince a manager to work with YOU? How do you demonstrate your proficiency, the ability to create value for them?
	MANAGERS: How do you select the right designer for a project? Which criteria do you apply?

Q5:	DESIGNERS: What are the biggest pain points/hurdles in the collaboration with a manager?
	MANAGERS: What are the biggest pain points/hurdles in the collaboration with a designer?
Q6:	DESIGNERS: How do you evaluate if a client is satisfied with a design solution?
	MANAGERS: How do you evaluate the quality of a design solution? Which criteria/KPI? How do you judge it?
→	Do you define common goals in the beginning?
Q7:	MANAGERS: How do you justify financial spending (expense/investment) on design?

III	Overcoming the "perception gap"
Q8:	What is needed to improve mutual understanding?

IV	The expectations of designers and managers (non-designers) from representatives
Q9:	Where could this help come from?

V	Quick win
Q10:	If you could change one circumstance right now – what would it be?

B. Guiding interview questions for design and business representatives

I	Level of awareness of the "perception gap" between designers and managers (non-designers)
Q1:	How can design contribute value to a business?
Q2:	How would you describe the relationship between designers and managers?
Q3:	Why do the two parties perceive the value of design so differently?

II	Overcoming the "perception gap"
Q4:	How could designers / managers get in touch with business / design culture / language?
→	What must be done by design and business education?
Q5:	What could be done to promote design as a strategic tool for value creation?
→	What must be done by design and business representatives?
Q6:	What are the biggest hurdles in bringing designers and non-designers together?

III	Quick win
Q7:	If you could change one circumstance right now – what would it be?